Mum went shopping. She took
the children.

The children looked up. There
was an elephant on the roof.

The elephant looked funny. The
elephant was fat.

The children laughed.
"Look at that fat elephant,"
they said.

"An elephant?" said Mum. "Don't be silly."

There was a storm. The wind blew.

It rained and rained.

It was a bad storm. The wind
was strong.

It blew the elephant away.

The children went to school. The elephant was in the playground.

The children laughed.

The children told Mrs May.
"Look at that fat elephant,"
they said.

"An elephant?" said Mrs May.
"Don't be silly."

The children liked the fat
elephant. They wanted it to
stay.

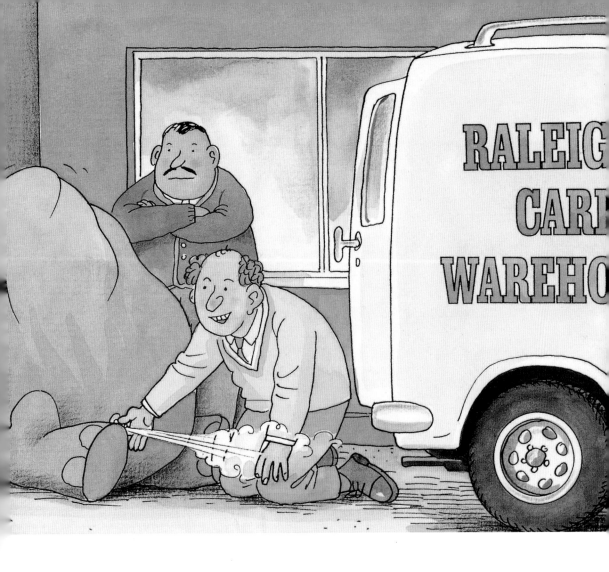

"Sorry," said the man. "We want
it back."

"Look at the fat elephant," said Biff.
"It's a flat elephant now," said Wilma.